This Sketchbook Belongs To:

_____

_____

_____

Enjoying this Notebook?

Please leave a review because we would love to hear your feedback, opinions and advice to create better products and services for you! Also, we want to know how you creatively use your notebooks and journals.

Thanks for your support!
You are greatly appreciated!

43238215R00064

Made in the USA
Middletown, DE
21 April 2019